nickelodeon

SQUAREPANTS

UNDERWATER FRIENDS

Popcorn
ELT
Readers

New Words

change colour

This animal **changes colour**.

foot / feet

deep

grumpy

He's **grumpy**.

land

Which animal lives on the **land**?

sleep

The dog is **sleeping**.

move

I can't **move**!

swim

She can **swim**.

Where's the popcorn?
Look in your book.
Can you find it?

UNDERWATER FRIENDS

This is SpongeBob. He is a sea sponge.
This is his home.

Sea sponges live underwater. A lot of sea sponges do not **move**!

Gary is a sea snail. He lives with SpongeBob.

Sea snails **move** very slowly. They have one big **foot**.

Patrick is a sea star. He likes to **sleep**.

Many sea stars have five **arms**. They can **move**. They have a lot of small **feet**.

feet

arm

Squidward is an octopus. He is **grumpy**.

Octopuses can **swim** fast. They can **change colour** too.

Mr Krabs is a crab. He loves **money**.

money

Crabs walk **sideways**. They live in the sea and on the **land**.

sideways

This is Pearl Krabs. She is a whale.

Whales are very big. Some whales can **swim** in very **deep** water.

Mrs Puff is a puffer fish. SpongeBob has classes in Mrs Puff's **boat**.

boat

A puffer fish is not very big ...

... or is it? Now it has water in its **stomach**.

stomach

This is Sheldon J Plankton. He is very small.
Sometimes SpongeBob does not see him.

There is a lot of plankton in the sea.
Fish and whales eat plankton.

After you read

1 Do the wordsearch.

 a ✓

 b

 c

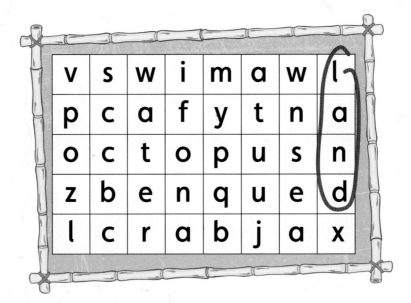

v	s	w	i	m	a	w	l
p	c	a	f	y	t	n	a
o	c	t	o	p	u	s	n
z	b	e	n	q	u	e	d
l	c	r	a	b	j	a	x

 d

 e

 f

2 Write the names.

~~plankton~~   sea snail   sea sponge   sea star   whale

a

p l a n k t o n

b

_ _ _   _ _ _ _

c

_ _ _   _ _ _ _ _ _

d

_ _ _ _ _

e

_ _ _   _ _ _ _ _

21

3 Circle the correct word.

a) **Puffer fish** / **Sea stars** have small feet.

b) **Octopuses** / **Whales** can change colour.

c) Many **crabs** / **sea stars** have five arms.

d) **Sea snails** / **Crabs** walk sideways.

e) Whales eat **plankton** / **sea sponges**.

Quiz time!

Answer the questions. Yes or No?

		Yes	No
1)	SpongeBob is a sea star.	☐	☑
2)	Squidward is always happy.	☐	☑
3)	Patrick likes to sleep.	☐	☐
4)	Mr Krabs loves money.	☐	☐
5)	Pearl Krabs lives with SpongeBob.	☐	☐

SCORES

How many of your answers are correct?

0-2: Read the book again! Can you answer the questions now?

3-4: You like SpongeBob and his friends!

5: Wow! Are YOU SpongeBob?

Chant

1 🔵 **Listen and read.**

The sea race

The crab walks sideways.
The octopus swims fast.
The sea sponge doesn't move
And the sea snail is always last!

2 🔵 **Say the chant.**